to ROSE BUDS;

Charleston, SC
www.PalmettoPublishing.com

to Rose Buds;
Copyright © 2023 by A. M. Orpel

All rights reserved

No portion of this book may be reproduced, stored in a retrieval system, or transmitted in any form by any means–electronic, mechanical, photocopy, recording, or other–except for brief quotations in printed reviews, without prior permission of the author.

Paperback ISBN: 979-8-8229-2862-6

to ROSE BUDS;

A. M. ORPEL

TABLE OF CONTENTS

SPRING — 1

The First Dinner	2
The Rain	3
Glass Menagerie	4
Don't Ask and I Won't Tell	6
Forget and Tell	8
You're) Cliché	10
Queer	12
Stained Memories	14
Crave You	16
Another Rose, I Suppose	18
Man on the Moon	20
To: The Man on the Moon	21
Snake Honey	22
Wind Chimes	24
The Garden and Its Leaves	25
Dew Drops	26
Anything But Perfect	28

Blue Faces	29
Flower Crowns	32
0:36	34

SUMMER — 37

Helpless. In Water	38
Broken Film	40
It's The Boys Who Wait	42
Force Fed	44
Unbothered	46
Pluto	47
Him	49
Sunset in a Cup	51
A Dark Night's Beauty	52
Cold Brew Candy	54
Your Tattoo	56
My Breath	59
Meant To Be	61
AJ	63
Content with being Content	64

Wildflowers	66
Yin	68
AUTUMN	71
Yang	72
Gasping for Air	74
to Rose Buds;	76
Black Orchid	78
To the person that deserves love,	80
Thoughts for a Rainy Day	82
Sociopath	83
Solitude is Pristine	85
Forever is Nothing	86
Truth	87
Peppermint Headaches	88
Keep My Blessings	90
Ophelia	92
Psychopath	94
One Sip	97
Here's a Portion of My Peace	99
Red Roses	101

WINTER 103

In Which It Needs 104
Shadowless 107
Sounds of the Orphanage 109
Words Spoken 111
What is the End? 113
(Darling) I Love You 115
Seasons 116
Room 392 118
Rzeka 120
Looks like 9 O'clock, Feels Like 5PM 122
Pain 123
Feel Nothing 125
We Can't Keep This Up 127
Hypothermia 129
May Death Do You a Favor 130
The Last Dinner 131

SPRING

THE FIRST DINNER

A time filled with grace.
Gifts and glory passed around the table.
Fires are set to dim
And snow is set to fall.
You smell the burning of pity,
White dreams fill the house.
Cars upon cars come up;
And there's no room left--
For you. As you keep driving.
Families gather, while grace is passed
Smiles and stories of the old are shared.
Then as the cars leave,
You come up.
Silence fills the halls,
And the dinners are set to end
Meanwhile, dreams are set to start.
The grace is remembered,
The times are forgotten.
And it's all... bullshit

THE RAIN

How dare you accuse me
To make the sweet heavens cry
I do not justify my reasonings
But life must go by

I give you joy
I allow you to feel it
How dare you blame me
For the despair you feel

I love and caress you
You are my child
I do not humble myself
Upon your greatness

I bring you life
And I let it prosper
I do not entice you
Your feelings have no meaning to me

But do not weep
When I bless you with tears from the sky
Do not belittle me
Because I can make it all stop.
I can take your pain away

GLASS MENAGERIE

Fresh starts,
A piece in my mind.
Of tiny little things
That make up my life

We think there's many
When there's one.
Seeing a thousand eyes
But none to look at

Pressing fingers against
Foggy glass in winter's time.
Keep your lips pursed
One whisper before the other

I can see the hills beyond me,
Burned til fresh starts.
Sparkles in the distance,
I'd love to watch you smile

Feelings of warm thread
Your laces are untied.
Keep your lips pursed
One thought at a time

A sun's last heartbreak,
Dawn brings fresh starts.
I'd hope you think of me
~A glass menagerie~

Don't Ask and I Won't Tell

Your secret's safe with me
Don't you ever worry
The truth will come out
When the dead man plays his game

Keep your lies
Tucked away in coat pockets
Each story
Tells a different one

Smirking away your problems
Winking away time
If only,
Dead men told tales

Secrets would fill your room
Out the hallway is the truth
Down the hall you go
And your lies follow

Look up and see
You might find something
Hidden away in dreams
Is the true life of mystery

Your secret's safe with me
You don't have to worry
Your truth will come out
When I decide to play

FORGET AND TELL

Honey, it's completely pointless
Honey, are you unaware
Darling, I'm completely pointless
Darling, you're still unaware

Secrets are to keep
Until little lies open up
Promises are to lose
Until deals are made

There is poison
In the words we say
Exquisite little thoughts
Are the price we pay

Who to trust
In the icy world
Break into conversation
Thaw out what you want to say

Tortured thoughts
Gone through battle
Enemies sort allies
And allies break free

Who to trust
What serendipity it is
When the right words
Fall into the wrong hands

In this world
We've come to know:
Sometimes,
Even the nicest snakes bite

YOU'RE) CLICHÉ

You're definitely sitting at home
Reading your favorite magazine
Sitting in your ripped jeans
Waiting for the world to turn

I know
We repeat things
It gets old
I know

Stolen groceries
In your nearby plaza
Milk in your hand
Leaving the freezer open

Prosthetic happiness
Shoes on your feet
You've got numbers to dial
I'll wait

Color dripping from your hands
Oceans of mystery
You've got snow in your brain
But please, don't let it get to waste

Baking your time away
Do you believe in destiny?
Some truths are meant to be told
But you don't quite have one

I'll wait
You can't help it
I always knew--
You were--
cliché

QUEER

In all of their group
There was one,
But two

They walk queer
As they stand tall
With their designer handbags

One holds the other
While those talk
Amongst themselves

And they walk in shadows
And talk of queer things
While thinking straight

They cuddle,
You can hear--
The laughter

I see them walking,
Right past me
As I stare in awe

Two women held hands
And I think,
That may have been
The queerest thing I saw

STAINED MEMORIES

Why are we going to hide it?

There's a million people around
How come, it's you that stands out?
Maybe you're different
Maybe you're not trying to hide

Or maybe you are
Perhaps you're just like everyone else
But something about you
It catches my eye

You're stained;
Virtually imperfect.
You're tainted,
And maybe that's it

Maybe that's why
Cause you don't hide.
You're virtually imperfect,
You're just my type

It just doesn't explain
The moment I'm feeling
The reasons I'm thinking
The way you stain me

You'll taint me,
As if I want to be tainted.
You may change me,
But on one condition

Perhaps you can show me
All your imperfections,
And give me a taste,
Of who you really are

Why are we trying to hide it?

CRAVE YOU

I might not speak again
And it's all due to you
I will sing the sad song
And I just wonder who--
Will be here tonight
At your crazy parties

You're so under-planned
You're so in command
You're so in demand
And no wonder he looks up to you

You're all I crave
There's so much I want to do
There's so much I need to do
If only you knew

You're with him
Cause you know that I hate him
And you're with her
Cause you know that she hates me
Cause you know I think about you
And I know that you think about me too

So screw what you do to me
Cause we both know
We both know that we're in love
We're in love with the wrong thing

How can you crave your fears?
How can you do what you do?
How can I do what you do?
Why do I still crave you?

Always at parties
Always in my favorite dress
Always staring across the room
During those big fancy dinners
Are you trying to get caught?
Is that the game you play?

I love what I shouldn't
I always burn in your fire
You get washed out by my love
I crave your desire

Give me your attention
I don't care anymore
Let's get caught
I'll always crave you anyway

Another Rose, I Suppose

Just one touch,
My love
You tease,
But do as you please

Movement on the Earth's surface
Bumps that face Mars
Marks that leave scars
Beautiful oceans

Motion, throughout
You can hear the heart beats
Blood is rushing
Adrenaline

Blooming in buds
We have lost something
That we--
Can never find

Outside,
Inside
Heat,
Then cold

A part of you
You tease,
My love,
But do as you please

Up by your window,
Just you in your clothes
It can wait
Another rose, I suppose

MAN ON THE MOON

I'm still waiting for that day
For that day, that day in May
Will you remember just what to say
On that evening, that evening in May

I'm still walking in the cold
Cause no matter what--
May's not close

You're still waving, me hello
When I told you, to let it go
Cause I've said goodbye
But, your heart is my gold

And what will happen--
When I sleep at noon
And what will happen--
When you wake up soon

I'll be awake, awake for you
You'll stay awake, awake for me
We'll both wave, and what we'll see--
Is just two lovers, you and me

TO: THE MAN ON THE MOON

That day in May had finally came
We waited so patiently
We waited for that day
For that day, that day in May

Are you still walking in the cold?
Cause no matter what--
I'm here to keep you warm

I'd still wave hello,
Even when you said to let it go
How'd you say goodbye
When you were my everything

What did happen--
When you slept at noon
And what did happen--
When I slept so soon

You stayed awake, awake for me
I stayed awake, and dreamed for you
We both waved and what they'll see
Is just the two lovers apart, just you and me

SNAKE HONEY

"Serendipity",
7 letters too long
"Honey",
7 letters too short

Exquisite,
Thawing out-
Ice. From-
Unwanted conversations

Snake,
Boiling poison
Honey,
Frozen wishes

Thaw out,
A life
You've been dreading
For years

You're searching
With a blindfold
When I'm right here
To find

Exquisite
By nature
You'll always be--
Serendipity

That is why,
"Honey",
Is 7 letters too short
"Honey, I'm yours"
Is 7 letters too perfect

WIND CHIMES

Where do you go when you walk away?
In a field of petals, you silently lay.
In your journey of excluding time
Following the sounds of wind chimes
In the cool meadows, the leaves sway

And over the hills, skies are gray
Raining into the river bay
In the ending days, a perfect crime
Where do you go?

Altering the path that stay
In the forgotten days of May
A lone mountain to climb
And nothing left to rhyme
In the end of long days
Where do you go?

THE GARDEN AND ITS LEAVES

The garden and its leaves;
May they fall to rest

In the times of winter and summer's eve
The moon slowly dawns upon me

The cool breeze, brings shadows
Until the light shines its glory

Twilight and morning become one
Troubled deer run along

The twisted forest calls out its name
And beauty is hidden within

She is elegant; the flowers begin to blossom
Spring must hear its calling

The sun travels miles across the valley
Stars await its arrival

Leaves begin to fall
The deers begin to rest

And then…
There is silence

Dew Drops

Crystal sunrises
Midnight walks
Busy streets
And talks with the moon

Petals and leaves
Down to your knees
Covered in love
Covered in blood

Let the dew drops come
From your broken eyes
Drip upon
The moonlit skies

Sleep alone
Rushing waters
Love was shown
In the name of our heavenly fathers

Vaseline on your lips
A drip and a sip
From the leaves that pour
A teary-eyed beach shore

Let the dew drops come
From your broken eyes
Drip upon
When leaves cry

Anything But Perfect

The scars across my body
The bleached out hair
The acne on my face
The people that stare

You place your hands upon my body
They're cold to the touch
Like frozen waves melting
Upon every inch

Damaged, both inside and out
Feeling the sensation
That death has to offer
It's called, "Intimidation"

Warped, like black stripes
The mark of ink
Deep breathing
And the eyes forget to blink

How do you touch my body?
How do you think I'm worth it?
To think I'm everything
When I'm, anything but perfect

Blue Faces

Imagine a world where everything was the same
We all wore the same shirt
We all sang the same tune
We all walked the same place
We all had a blue face
No one was unique
No one would stand out
Parents just nodded
And schools gave handouts
They say, "be normal"
They say, "go with the crowd"
They say, "don't be a freak"
They say, "make yourself proud"
But how can I be proud
when I'm like the rest
How can I make sense
when I don't have my own zest
I say this world needs a little color
This world needs difference
Cause if only you knew
How it is to be blue

Being blue isn't nice
You have to hide it with a mask
To show the world that you're happy
Cause you're stuck with an endless task
This society isn't real
People hide just what they feel
So people run and steal
So no one is allowed to heal
But you don't care about the blue
Cause it has nothing to do with you
But I'll tell you it's horrible
And I'd never wish it against you
Cause to feel it too
Would be your worst nightmare
A sad sickening thing
Cause being blue isn't fair for you
It shouldn't be with anyone
But people are forced to have it
From people who hurt them
People who don't care
But you'll never see their true faces
And you'll never truly understand
All I've done for you

And yet you still make me feel blue
Why should I feel this way?
Why should people stay the same?
Going through all this hate
Why can't we say what we want to say
I'd say, "rise up"
I'd say, "be different"
I'd say, "be *you*"
I'd say, "you're gallant"
And you don't need the pain
You should just let you be you
Cause all you can do for me--
Is just let me become happy

FLOWER CROWNS

You and your teenage depression
Spending your time thinking
Fidgeting with pens and pencils
When you know you'd rather be drinking

The sun skims through your room
It decides you're a waste of time
So you sit back and relax
Knowing that you'll be just fine

The yard is out calling you
The leaves feel your heart trembling
The north writes your name in the stars
It's in your smile, resembling

Footprints made of glue
Your room is such a mess
Your fingers feel the fidgeting
I can tell you're in distress

But I can tell,
There's more you want
As I see you come around
It's me that you taunt

I'll show you a secret
At the edge of the town
Come away with me
We can make flower crowns

0:36

'brb'
I'll be right back
Kinda lost in my mind right now

...

Sorry I couldn't get there,
My mom went shopping for groceries
And I stood in the strawberry aisle
As my thoughts went

        r

        a

        m

        p

        a

        n

        t

I)... Don't worry,
I noticed. your new shoes
I wonder,

Is that why you called?

Please,
Leave a message
After'the   tone

                           ...

SUMMER

HELPLESS. IN WATER

I saved a helpless bee today
It was drowning in my pool
I looked at it and thought,
"Maybe I'd like to drown too"

I saw it twisting and turning
Looking for life
Memories and burning
Upon the moonlight

Smiles within frowns
And frowns within smiles
I was happy
But that hasn't been for awhile

A family you're not a part of
Strangers to come home to
Maybe it'd be easier
If one day... I didn't come

I saved a helpless bee today
It was drowning in my pool
Soon it flew home, but all I could think was,
"What if I drowned too"?

Broken Film

Chinese bed shops
And Italian tea
Barber shops for men
And beauty parlors for women

Black and white love
With grey in between

Speaking in tongues
Laughing in the same tone
A broken marriage
And no kids to come home to

Grey mixed sheets
With black and white in between

People stay on repeat
Like the records we used to play
On aisle 5
Looking for our sanity

Shades we live in
With no color in between

We taste sweet
In a bitter wasteland
But look at you
All dollied up

We've been drained of it all
I see the black in your eyes; between

And the gentlemen
Go to play
With wives at home
Hiding simple truths

We can't wait for the day
When the people can't hide between--

The broken film

IT'S THE BOYS WHO WAIT

The boys who sit--
At the kitchen table
And listen to the screams

With eyes
On the back of their heads
And the cries
Flowing down their necks

It is July
In the middle of the day
Grass is green
But the boys are locked away

And bloodshot
Is all they see
And footsteps
Is all they hear

They want to run
To the farthest of valleys
And the nearest of trees

To feel the wet grass
And swing to the top of the world
To sneak to freedom
To let them be

They try to escape
With the quickest of footsteps
We try to escape
With the smallest of thoughts

Blood running down--
Their rosy cheeks
The stains stay on
The carpet not clean

Bruises
And quivering lips
Pressed upon things

They are beaten and broken
The boys at the table
In the middle of July
In the middle of their life
It's the boys who wait

FORCE FED

Smoke behind your eyes
Raging fires put out
Caving from domestication
You're stuck unsatisfied

Soaking up the sun
And feeding little lies
Childish views on politics
And political views on children

Take your eyes back home
And sing yourself to sleep
Mind full of loneliness
Hunger left unclean

Different thoughts
From those of your lover's
Psychopathic, mixed
With a little, psychotic

Ease into new tastes
Lying is the best experience
Taste buds burn up
When the fog is cleared

Feed little lies
Plant them in your garden
Shed a tear
And the truth just might start to grow

UNBOTHERED

Sometimes I want to lay in the sun
I want to feel the breeze,
But I hate grass
I want to lie where the world can't get me
And listen to songs on repeat
I want to breathe clearly
And sing as if I've got talent
I want my friends to know that they hurt me
And my family to know I don't love them
I want to have everything
And make myself proud
I want to hang my posters up
And never clean the house
I just want to lie in the street
And never get up

Pluto

The moon and the stars do not reach you

Watching from the sidelines,
It's game day.
All the big names walk out,
And there you are;
The lonely photographer.

When all the kings and queens gather,
You are the jester of all things.
You brought yourself to it,
And you're the only one who will

You snap here and you snap there,
You capture the memories.
But that's all they are,
They don't care who's behind the film

The actors are in play
And the writers are merely forgotten.
You have a pen and a pencil,
Yet everyone else claims they can write

We're in the last few minutes
They all turn to see
Lights fill the arena
Then all of sudden;
It's dark.

And the moon and stars do not reach
you anymore

HIM

What I think about most
--Is his coffee stain
I laugh

What he thinks about most
--Is my smile
He laughs

What I think he knows
--Something I can't tell him
He frowns

What he thinks I know
--My own secrets
I frown

What is paradise?
--Here is my silence
I am quiet

What is his paradise?
--Her
I am gone

What are your regrets?
--That day
Silence

And what do you miss?
--Him
There is only... silence

Sunset in a Cup

A day breaks
Like the crack in a cup
So still,
Yet so fragile

A day in heaven
Your french vanilla creamer
Sugar waves
And melted ice

Clouds and the rain
Pouring like a river
A stain on the carpet
From twenty years ago

Sweet memories
Melt your taste buds
Your glass--
Is almost empty

A disarray of lights--
Strung up in the sky
The day has set.
God has finished his coffee

A Dark Night's Beauty

She's got coffee-colored sandals
Underneath her pale moon feet
She's got too many angels
Dancing to her beat

She is a dark night's beauty
And a mid day's nightmare
She will be your last goodbye
But a first goodnight

Bright blue eyes
Under all that red heat
Dark blue headaches
From last night's creep

She can put your life together
And she'll rip it right from you
And she'll do it with a smile
Cause she knows it'll hurt for a while

You can walk in the green-blue meadow
And she can walk in the deepest hell
You can ask her how she's doing
And she'd say, "well"

She's a trap in disguise
But you'd still love her
Rainbows and grays
Never any delays

Always free spirit
Even in the den of night
Such a lonely fool
Such a lonely beauty

COLD BREW CANDY

She tastes like cold brew candy

Her hair out the window
Part of the sunset
Reds and oranges
Bright blue, yellow

Waves like the Dead Sea
Floating on top of everything
Down to her back
Flowing to shore

Salty then sweet
An unappreciated appetite
Warm in the morning
Cool in the evening

A storm's brewing--
A sweet memory
Frosty--
With the undertones

Spit out
Onto this cold floor
Left for nothing
Dead for something

I bet she tastes like cold brew candy

YOUR TATTOO

Always in that red dress
That goes down to your knees
What're you trying to show?
Cause I know what I'm trying to see

Why do you do that slow dance
With the boy that she loves?
Why do you undress
With the boys downstairs?

You know what your mother would say?
And do you know what your father would do?
If they only knew what you were up to
If they only knew I was with you

Late at night
You know I'm not trying to hide
Are you up at night?
We both know that you are

We both know about your tattoo
The one you were told not to get
It's on your back
I'm the only one who knows it

I was with you
Out in the rain
You yelled
I was blamed

And we both know how I saw
I was with your bra
And it wasn't only a tattoo
There was also a bruise

Isn't that why you yelled that day?
You were mad
You didn't get your way
And I was mad…
But I was blamed

I'd never give you that
And I wish I didn't know--
Who gave it to you
But, I'd never hurt you

But we both know how I saw
You had no bra
But that's not what I need to see
When your dress goes down to your knee

My Breath

I lie at the bottom of the ocean
I am completely alone
This. is. solitude.

There is wake.
Until I was up on shore
And feel the sandy beaches

There you were
Out of nowhere
My breath-

I can see the fog forming
Your footprints match mine
But, you're not here

Feelings of fading
I begin to sink
Back into your arms-

Until I wake up
I want to face you
Even if it's the last time

But there you were
Standing on the ocean floor
When my lips met yours

Now I know
Out of nowhere,
A breath of fresh air

It was like-
I could finally;
.Breath Again.

Meant to Be

We were dancing in the rain
On that sweet ol' holiday
When he pulled out all those games
And drank his sweet old champagne

We would play out in the yard
He was driving his old car
Creating his own kind of sweet talk
Lovin' things we do

Remember at the movies
When we got drunk on smoothies?
How did we remember that
At the party?

We came up on a Monday
Sold it all on Sunday
Drank up all our money
But we were still meant to be

Even if they hate me
Sayin' that I hate you
But isn't that what we do
While dancing in the rain?

Cause we were dancing in the rain
On that sweet ol' holiday
We're talking our own sweet talk
Lovin' things we do

AJ

A late night raspberry
On summer nights
So much left to say
So much left unspoken
In ways we act
Unrecognizable figures
Where does this night end?
You make me want to say things,
But how do I say--

I love you?

CONTENT WITH BEING CONTENT

Monumental
It's one word to describe
How feelings
Play a part
In every role

Am I really okay?
It's almost a feeling of loneliness.
Coming from nothing
To having all--
That I want

It makes you crazy
Just the thought of it
I've begun a bad habit
And I'm not too sure
Why?

I create problems
To distance the problems.
I create negativity
To distract
My positivity

The truth being--
I'm not too sure how to express
All of the feelings
That I feel
With being content

I am beyond happy
Yet I fill myself a void
To avoid what I'm feeling
It's almost unreal
It's almost lonely

Sometimes it's hard
Am I content with being content?
Is happiness so hard?
Because I AM happy,
But will I truly allow it

I have fallen so hard
All I want to do is keep falling
But myself is stopping me
And I find that--
I'm right back, to where I was

But I can believe
I will believe.
I am content
With being content
If I am content with you

WILDFLOWERS

Seven story building--
At high noon
The things you see--
Across the street

....

You always told me
You liked wildflowers
That the sun hand picked
For butterflies to carry

And when they dropped
You wished you'd catch one
To feel the saying
"There are butterflies in your stomach"

Always in the past
Reading your memories
'Let's run around in suits
And take black and white photos'

I have your Polaroid
That has one picture
You smiled, looking back
As if I were still coming

I look across the street
Butterflies fill the air
Wildflowers intertwined
It's too bad, that I'm not outside

YIN

There's always a side
To one story
Always a pin
To each point

I was in love with you
With a side
To my own story

New decisions make up my day
However,
It's always the outcomes--
I don't like

I still remember
Every cool night
When our fingers pressed together
And we would hold tight

Onto each other
You were a beauty in disguise
However,

I feel every point
That your body holds.
Every mark, every hour
I feel you

Sometimes I miss it
All the long nights,
Talking,
Waiting...

I miss the way you looked at me
The way you ran to my arms
However,
I don't like it

The outcomes of your story
Become a pin in mine
Sometimes I wish...
You left just fine.

AUTUMN

YANG

There's always two sides
To the same story
Always a pin
For each point

I was in love
With your side
Of our story

New decisions made up my day
However,
The consequences always--
Ruined it

Do you remember
The warm nights
When our hands fit perfectly
Holding so tight

With one another
You were the beast to my beauty
However,

I miss every point
That you made to me
All the fights, all the silence
I felt you

Every moment I miss it,
Your eyes looking at me,
Watching,
Waiting...

I miss seeing you from a distance
When I kept running to your arms
However,
You never caught me

The consequences of my story
Became a pin in yours
Sometimes I just wish...
I had lived to see it become "ours".

GASPING FOR AIR

She never thought you liked paint
Yet you smeared it all over your face
As if in this day and age
You were ready for war

Unlike the rest of us
You brought the war
Unlike her
You were the war

Dollied up brunette
Eating lunch across the table
Eyes met
And who would've known?

Who would've known?
That the world would come crashing down
Who would've known?
Who would've ever really known?

But like the war
It brings heartache
It brings terror
It brings an end to all things

But you'd never know
If you sat across the table
When the eyes meet
But the soul rests uneasy

In the end of the war
Thoughts are left awake
Air is left breathless
But yet you still gasp for it

Silence fills the fields
Of the two whose eyes met
But the words that filled the air
Can come from a time remembered

Back when the fields were clear
And the skies weren't black
And maybe if you listen close enough
You might just hear something back

TO ROSE BUDS;

"It's complicated"
I said
To you, to me
Over 2000 miles
Of love

12,000 hugs
4 kisses goodbye
Phone calls goodnight
Alone by your bedside

Prayers
And plane flights
Football,
Drive bys
In the moonlight

They're rose buds
Made of plastic fillings
Looks to be real
But made to last forever

A small town,
But movie theater love
You're alone now.
But that won't stop

10 unread messages
4 kisses goodbye
Phone calls at night
His picture, at your bedside

...

"It's complicated"
You said

No,
"They're simply rose buds
Made of plastic fillings
What looks to be real...
But was made to last forever"

Black Orchid

Melt into my hands
And drip onto the carpet
Play your melody
And drink like the bands

Crippled by life
Don't bother with me
I gave you it all
Growing into the world

What is meant to be?
Lace yourself on me
Beauty at its finest
Lace yourself on thee

A black orchid--
Is all you leave
A black orchid--
Is all I grieve

It was your favorite
And I miss all of you
Not just the parts you left
But even all the rest

I miss your feel
Black orchid
Lying there
Just horrid

A black orchid
Is all you leave behind
Just...A black orchid
It'll leave you blind

TO THE PERSON THAT DESERVES LOVE,

I'm sorry
That the world died
And along
You died with it

I'm sorry
That you hurt
And I wish
I could take that away

I'm sorry
That I keep in my feelings
And waste your day
When you're down

I'm sorry
And you may not know why
Sometimes my feelings
Can't be expressed by words

But if it would help
I would tell you every day
Just how much
I loved you

I'd tell you
Everyday
But I'm afraid
To get hurt

I'm so afraid
That love
Would make you leave
Again

Thoughts for a Rainy Day

Burning
A silhouette
In the eye view

Closing in
Reaching out
To the outskirts

A dreamy oasis
Left to the Skies
A desert equation
In the eye of the mind

Numbness
It's. All. Around. You.
You're empty

Like everything else
Disappearing
From past mistakes

Oh how we wonder,
Does a tree still make sound
If it falls in empty woods?

SOCIOPATH

Feel the tension as it rises,
Feel the tension as it grows.
Feel the calm that isn't there,
Feel the calm as it leaves and goes.

Feel the tension,
Pop, pop, pop.
Feel the tension,
Stop, stop, stop.

Feel the heartbreak,
Feel the pins,
Feel the wood--
Of the broken stake.

Feel, feel, feel
Every word you say
Inch, inch, inch
Till I break away

Needles, come upon the skin
Blood, blood, blood
Pour, pour, pour
Till I feel I have no more

Feel the tension
Feel the ache
Feel till the day I wake

I, I, I
You, you, you
I feel the tension
You feel the pain

Shore, shore, shore
The water's still red
Pour, pour, pour
Till I feel no more

Solitude is Pristine

All nice and neat
(Why are they staring at me?)
Dress all clean and pristine
(I wish I was still seventeen)

Only me, myself, and I
(I wish I was a part of them)
Lying in the eye-
(Of a blind storm)

Smooth and steady
(I don't feel alive)
Easy rolling
(It's all just a game to survive)

Friends and more friends
(They think they know you)
Ends meet ends
(All alone in a crowd)

I lay
(All clean and pristine)
In solitude
(I wish they would stare at me)

FOREVER IS NOTHING

Cashed out dreams,
Pre-self esteem.
Bleached out hair
And beached out waves

Pre-existing conversations
A different matter of time
Those who go out
And those who stay put

Teeth are coming in
Friends are going out
Dreams are created
And flaws start early

The docks are empty
Light is filled with dark
Skate shops have left me
And there's not much left to do

Looking at the past--
Back when time mattered
Nothing is forever
And forever is nothing

TRUTH

I never
Even truly
Loved you

Peppermint Headaches

Out of a window,
We stare in the horizon
Hoping for the sky to turn
And for us to see it

The world is crashing down
In slow motion
In the blink of an eye
Movement ever so steady

And the lady in white
Drops her platter
But alas we stay,
Forever so still

An adrenaline rush
That hit our twenties
Delaying our time,
But we'd never forget
And we'd never go back
Restarting is a failed man's consequence

We've got a forever secret
Hidden away
In the midst of our childhood
Swimming in the lakes of mystery

Children singing
As the world came crashing down
We watch it all
As we are forever so still

KEEP MY BLESSINGS

I've never been a fan,
A fan of the court,
The court that we call--
"Church".

So I give you all my blessings,
No matter what they might be.
So keep it to yourself,
And you might just be in luck.

You should hear my warnings.
I can be very vague,
But I keep it to myself,
Every single day.

I keep the drama,
The drama that I yearn to spill,
So someone can hear me.
Please keep me still.

Cause I'm trapped in this cage.
I put on a face,
A face to face the world,
The world that we live in.

So I give you all my blessings.
To whom they shall receive.
They might have my lies,
Or they might have goodbyes.

I don't quite remember,
But I still encounter,
Everything I once felt,
A long long time ago.

So take up my knowledge,
Like you took up my brain.
I still think about you,
Every single day.

So I give you all my blessings,
And I hope you will get them.
Cause they contain my feelings,
All the things I *was* dreaming.

OPHELIA

Do you know why we picked orchids
Out in the field one day?
They were white,
But black to the touch

A golden mystery
With your name written on it
Weeks after that
You showed up

Something new about you
It always made me smile--
In awe.
And stare

In my precinct
In that famous red dress
Playing a dangerous game
In the field, that one day

Your tattoo,
Never seen before
I hadn't guessed--
It'd be
The black orchid
Your black orchid

Who knew,
That tears--
Could kill--
The thing you loved most.

One day you're going to walk
Far away from here
In a field of flowers
With your name written on it

And in the end
Why do you always leave...

A black orchid?

Psychopath

...

The difference between us is...
Well there's not much of a difference
Now is there?
Or we'd notice

I think we'd notice--
The dirty countertops
Or perhaps--
The blood in the freezer

Would we notice?
Or maybe we'll sit back,
And let it be
I'll lay upon your shoulder

...

The difference between us...
I can look you in the eye and smile
Maybe you'd smile back
That would make all the difference--

Wouldn't it?
If I knew you--
The way you knew you,
Things would be much different

Water would be colder
The house would appear much the same
But deep inside,
I am not familiar with the scent

...

The difference is...
I have no way of knowing--
What the cries of children--
Sound like

But perhaps, that is just me
I know you met someone new
I saw him the other day
It makes me think,

I've always liked the number three,
How bout you, Maria?
I say this
As I sit outside your window

...

ONE SIP

Alone. With a flame
All hope. Cause I don't feel
Freedom. In anguished lies
Freedom, lies inside

Melt. With loneliness
A feeling so shocking--
You couldn't dream.
You could never dream

Sighs,
In place of feelings
Hear your heart beating
For the first and last time

Take a deep breath
And close your eyes
Imagine your childhood home
But you can't remember

You could never remember

We almost forgot
Our iced tea
In line to drink
Like it's the first

How is it that we feel--
The blood in our veins
When we don't feel--
Anything?

Win a prize at the counter
See yourself. So precious.
When your eyes gave light
In dark places

Now. You're numb
Moving. The world awaits you
Freedom. In anguished lies
Freedom, isn't this what you asked for?

HERE'S A PORTION OF MY PEACE

I wish for a fair system
I wish for us to get--
The love that we deserve

To see the almighty man in the sky
To know that you've got someone watching --you
But not paying no attention to you

Finding out the reason behind hiccups
Finding out the reason behind lies
Or leaving an untold truth

Know the sounds from strings
Know the sounds dispersed in nature
Laugh with a frown on your face

See the colors of your hair
See the colors from the waves
Yet you choose to change it

Get organized with friends
Get sorted out with enemies
You play on both sides

Hear the whack on a racket
Hear the blood rushing to your head
Pass out and sleep

Daze away in space
Daze in colorful smoke
Live above the heavens

Drown out your sorrows
Drown out the sentiments
Pass out …and sleep.

RED ROSES

Flowers lain
Engulfing life
Rest aside
You will be fine

Her arms around them
Pricks on her fingers
Blood in her palms
Tears in her eyes

Her cut lips
And her cut hair
Made to look neat
While she's on her way

Lying there
Flowers lain
Pay our respects
Walk away

Petals fall
"Does she love me?
Does she love me not?"
Our sick games

Stay here,
Stay behind
You keep leaving
Stay in my mind

Leave your piece
Dirt stained
I'll see you again
Your flowers lain

WINTER

IN WHICH IT NEEDS

She needed that
The thing you stole
Now she's gone
It's cut a hole

We breathe
We drink
We eat
We live

But then we don't
But then we can't
We need it
But we can't have it

We live
We eat
We drink
We breathe

But some don't
She didn't
You don't
I don't

What do we want
Isn't what we get
Isn't what we need
Isn't our life

We breathe
We eat
We drink
And we don't

Let me live
Let me cry
What I need
Is my life

We breathe
We don't
We need
I leave

He's starving
Alone at night
She's thirsty
It's so bright

We don't
We need
We leave
We breathe

That is the last
That we need
We don't live
We don't eat
We don't drink
We can't breathe

Shadowless

Crying in the night
Hopeless and sad
It had been such a violent fight
Now a being in the dark
Searches for people
But sees no one
The town deserted
No lights, no food, nothingness
It had done no harm
But it is angry at who did
The man came in, counted to 10
Found the children, and took them in
He took them into his van
Past the houses, bridges, and mountains
The man did not see him
The boy in the corner
The boy knew why he wasn't seen
He is a ghost and is still living
He saw a woman on the ground
Lying in the dark, lifeless
She fought the man with all her strength

But was not strong enough to beat him
The boy was only now a shadow,
Blending in the dark
He is sad and guilty
He could only watch
Once he was a hero
Now lost
The boy stays in that town
The town by the ocean and woods
The town by the river and trees
The town that is deserted except for he

Sounds of the Orphanage

I stare in the mirror
My beauty does not reach my face
Like an hourglass stuck in time
Beauty forgets it's mine

Time will keep flowing
Down the sands of the desert
Filled with nothing but silence
Scream but nothing comes out

In a home full of strangers
That have your last name
Memories of a time
That never came

The ears ring
Like the telephones from long ago
There's a story of our past
We've yet to know

I feel the pavement on my feet
Water is gifted from the sky
Sounds fill the earth
Remembering old tales

Letters are sent
They are filled with sound
Memories from an old decade
Are filling my plate

Where have we heard this?
Where have we gone?
Memories from a place
A place since been erased

Words Spoken

I am beaten and broken
Left without my wings
My words have been stolen
I'm not able to speak

I wish that they knew--
The thoughts that go on
My brain is too cluttered
And I'd like it to stop

They claim to be me
"Oh the cruelty"
Stealing what's mine
Stealing my mind

But they know not,
Of the effort I give
They know not,
Of the pain I'm in

It may not be of the touch,
But the words I'm given
Through my ears--
It's the words I've heard

It has made me--
The way that I am
They have ruined--
Everything that I was

I am beaten and broken
Left without my wings
My words have been stolen
I'm not able to speak

WHAT IS THE END?

I am unable to forget,
What was once taught.
I am unable to remember,
What was once learned.

It all goes by so quickly.
What do they expect me to know?
It's the end of my life.
And so what do they expect me to know?

I'm caught between the chains;
The chains of life;
This so-called event,
That ruined everything.

I don't come by,
Or what has come by me,
The opportunities--
Have passed on.

I no longer feel
What everyone talks about
I no longer see
All of the doubt

My life is dead
And no one's around me
I can't see it anymore
And I don't know what's around me

I'm going numb
They can't see me
I'm going down
You can't see me

The world belongs to me
And now what
I've become a mess
Disown me

I feel nothing
You can't see me
I'm going numb
I can't see me...no more

(DARLING) I LOVE YOU

There's a part of me--
That wants to cry.
It hurts just so very much.
that i love you
But I see your past self
I see something that I wasn't part of
And when I look into the future,
There's nothing more I want
Then to see your smile
But you're not there
And you're not gonna be there
I listen to Snow Patrol in my room
And watch sappy love shows
I want to know the part of you--
That everyone else knows
Who's that girl who wears beanies?
Where's the girl who loved theater?
I want to know your middle name
And scream at your window late at night
You make me want to cry
Because, we'll never be like that
We'll never be in love
And it just hurts so very much
Because,
i still love you

SEASONS

I've been trying to tell you…

What?

"All things happen for a reason
Some people fall in love with the wrong season
And all the matches turn to grey
When we live in a black and white decay

Storms of old
And prayers new
I had one heart
And I gave it to you.

But some people walk away
And some people choose to stay
I disappointed them all
And it was you that made me fall

Sometimes I thought you were summer
But I still loved the cold weather
Even if the frostbite hurt me
You and I were made together.

But the world is a sad place
Filled with hope and tragedy
And sometimes I just wished
You know what had happened to me.

You're the only reason
I fell in love...
With all the seasons"

ROOM 392

My brain is a breeding ground for nonsense

I see white molecules everywhere I look
I think I see my blood in the air
Of troubles caused mentally
But I see it... Physically

There are shooting stars
And I hear the sounds of the sirens
Calling my name,
But just a distant... illusion

White restraints--
They are not molecules.
Red lights,
There is no longer... the blood

Needles pressed deep,
You can almost feel it.
But the wind is so strong,
It's really just... a reflection

And when you've got it all mapped out
The stars realign
And you see things blurry
Not realizing... this is truth.

But what is real and what is not?
When your brain is a breeding ground
for nonsense

RZEKA

I am stuck in the deadly cold.
With no place to call home.
They left me for dead.
And I've lost all hope.

If I ever return, I shall die for the best.
I expect the least.
I learn the most.
And I have seen death.

It is no longer the cold that bothers me.
It's the silence I've come to learn.
It's the beast that's waiting for me.
It's the beast that lives inside me.

My lungs have cut off oxygen.
I no longer have the will to breathe.
The water that is trapped.
The water that I'm trapped in.

I can feel it.
It's no longer cold inside.
He's waiting.
And I've nowhere to hide.

I remember only so little.
I was happy on the shore.
But, I sank away.
And I'm here to stay.

My bones can feel it.
And I can't feel my bones.
I have become the cold.
It's of the stories I've told.
I am one with the water.
And the water is one with me.
I feel no cold.
I am of the stories you've told.

LOOKS LIKE 9 O'CLOCK, FEELS LIKE 5PM

Trigger warnings,
Written in the snow.
The elk feed
And the men stay low

Where's the horizon
And the minute meals?
Our faces sweat
We forget to feel

My father came,
And his father too
We don't make the rules,
But we know who do

Woodsy cabin
Woods then cabin
Those that get left behind--
Don't speak, they *have* been

White without snow
Sitting on the roof
I see my brothers
Men who weren't bulletproof

PAIN

Oh, the pain you've caused me
The pain I shall receive
The pain that doesn't go away
The pain that wants to stay

It rots up inside me
It festers inside my soul
I can't release it
It burns like coal

The ashes left behind my eyes
The eyes that won't ever cry
To cry is to be weak
And being weak, just can't be

Pain shouldn't be bottled, though
Eventually, the bottle will flow
Over the top, the anger will spill
Spill onto the ones that make us feel

I wish the pain would go away
The pain that makes people shy from me
The trust issues I've gained
The people I've lost through the way

Pain is like a broken road
Not fixed, but left alone
It stays with you, until a new--
Person will fix you

FEEL NOTHING

Pre-existing adaptations
Lost in your mind
Feeling the need
To be the better one

It is not your fault
And I do not blame you
For if we wanted to speak truth
Our mouths would be open

Fragile memories
In accosting dreams
What is left
Of the thoughts we know?

See through
A glass window
The palm of your hand
Has feeling

No feeling
Is felt
On winter nights
Dew on leaves (left)

It wouldn't hurt
If we could feel

Nothing

WE CAN'T KEEP THIS UP

All this love
All this pain
I've felt for you
You never felt for me

You claimed you had
That you had it all
Without the need of me
So you threw me out

I saw it coming
Something you can't see for now
But you'll be in pain
The pain I still feel

Cause you chose *her*
Over me
Cause you chose death
Over peace

And I never loved you
Not in the way that you wanted
And maybe that's why
That's why you left

Cause I couldn't play the game
Play the game you control
The game I don't like
The game you still play

You play with hearts
You played with mine
I thought I could trust you
But you let it break

Cause you couldn't handle my truth
And the truth is, I couldn't handle you
Cause you're mean and stubborn
Cause you never believed me

And I hope that you miss me
Because you deserve that..at least
And I hope you realize
You can't fix what you ruined

HYPOTHERMIA

The waves in the ocean
The soft sound they make
A cold splash on your face
Now you're finally awake

Looking down the horizon
Lost in an endless space
Wanna be lost
With the endless frost

Feeling cool temperatures
Climbing down your back
Stuck in the motion
Now we're back at the ocean

Your mysteries--
Are out there
Your dreams,
....Your self esteem

Washing up on shore
Gone to the touch
Now this time,
There is no wake

May Death Do You A Favor

We lay
On a bed of roses
Soft texture
Soft mind

And we feel
The earth beneath us
Through our fingers
Through our toes

The warmth is drained
And the cool seeps in
From ahead
And from below

Sinking, together
We're alone
In death
In departure

With roses
We bleed
Go to sleep
Go to sleep

THE LAST DINNER

A time for the people to gather
While ways part ways.
All the skies can be seen,
Miles become dark upon lit highways
Snowfall has just begun
And you're just in time,
To hear the laughter, the joy.
Moonlit shadows call in the night
The cold fills the warm air.
The streets bare empty
And the shop-shine dims.
Holiday singing goes silent,
While the black dreams fill your head
Stories and memories fade in and out;
You drive. The cars fill the spaces.
You see the steamed glass,
The faces are rosy and clean
Your ways part theirs, so simple.
It's all you've ever dreamed of...
so simple

www.ingramcontent.com/pod-product-compliance
Lightning Source LLC
LaVergne TN
LVHW092050060526
838201LV00047B/1316